The Alphabet Takes a Journey: Destination Ethiopia

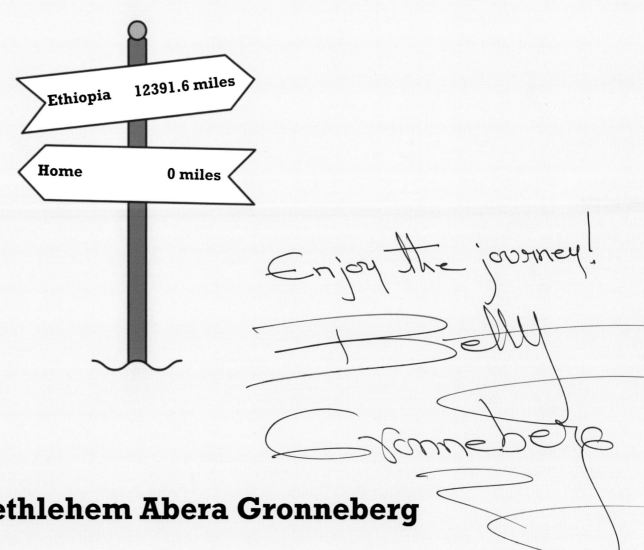

Ethiopia   12391.6 miles

Home   0 miles

Enjoy the journey!

Betty
Gronneberg

Written by Bethlehem Abera Gronneberg

To my sons - my rainbows:

Joshua / ጆሽዋ**/**
Gabriel / ጌብርኤል**/**
Nathaniel / ናታንኤል**/**

Ancient parchment in Geez from the church of Saint Mary of Zi...

Written and designed by Bethlehem Gronneberg.
www.bethlehemgronneberg.com

Library of Congress Control Number: 2015938638

First Edition printing, 2015.
Published by Prairiewood Press
ISBN-13: 978-0-692-42689-0
ISBN-10: 0692426892

Printed in China through Pettit Network Inc.
Asia Pacific Offset

The Journey Begins

It was a bright, beautiful September day,
when the English Alphabet gathered to say,
"We must explore, go across the deep blue sea,
To find other unique scripts and where they could be."

The Alphabet pondered and conjured some plans
To embark on a journey, explore other lands.
"Destination Ethiopia!" it was decreed.
An ancient land of splendid beauty, indeed.

Upon arrival to this foreign land,
They saw lots of letters, but of a different brand.
They were astonished. "Wow! What a crowd!
We can't wait to hear you all sounding out loud."

The Ethiopian letters - the Amharic Feedel,
All 200 plus of them, were surprised too.
"So many of us, so few of you."
Each Amharic letter extended a hand
And sang in unison, "Welcome to our land!"
The plan was explained: Each letter shown around
By Amharic Feedel families of that letter's sound.

"Let's go explore!" the tour guides grinned.
The letters replied, "Let the journey begin!"

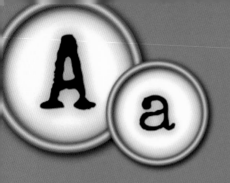

አ/uh/ ኡ/oo/ ኢ/ee/ ኣ/ah/ ኤ/ay/ እ/eh/ ኦ/oh/

At the airport, letter A was greeted by the first Feedel family. "Allow me to introduce my siblings," said አ/uh/, the oldest. Then, all at once, the seven forms of A lined up in a row to be sounded out: አ/uh/ ኡ/oo/ ኢ/ee/ ኣ/ah/ ኤ/ay/ እ/eh/ ኦ/oh/

"We are in the capital city, *Addis Ababa*," explained ኡ/oo/. "*Addis Ababa* means 'new flower' in the Amharic language. It is our largest city with over four million people. "

"We live at the foothills of the mountains surrounding the city," added ኢ/ee/ as they roll through the city in a taxi. "If you feel short of breath right now, there is a good reason for it. *Addis Ababa* is built on a very high elevation. One of the world's highest capital cities.'"

Along the way, ኤ/ay/ taught letter A some cheerful Amharic words. "In our language, if I add '-ye' to the end of your name, it means I like you and I am comfortable with you." And then ኤ/ay/ added, "Does that make sense, A-ye?" At this, letter A smiled bashfully.

Airplane / አውሮፕላን **(aw-RO-plan)**
this giant bird of Africa, soars higher than the clouds,
through many miles and children's smiles,
it flies and wows the crowds.

B b

/ʌ/buh/ ʌ·/boo/ ʌ/bee/ ʌ/bah/ ʌ/bay/ ʌ·/beh/ ʌ/boh/

A cup of tea and freshly baked bread was served for breakfast at the home of the ʌ/buh sound family.

"Today, adventure awaits!" broadcasted ʌ·/boo/, second in command of the troop. So they flew to the town of *Gondar* to start their hike up the *Semien* mountains.

At the meadows of these high mountains live a colony of gelada baboons, commonly known as the 'bleeding heart' monkeys or the 'lion monkeys' because of their look.

Letter B and ʌ·/boo/ helped each other climb stiff cliffs. They huffed and they puffed but they kept on their trekking task. As the mountains rose, so did their wish to reach the final peak.

At long last an amazing sight revealed, breathtaking views and a sea of monkeys! Too many to count, too many to keep track. "What an adventure indeed!" exclaimed B.

Next stop, the Blue Nile Falls. It is nicknamed "water that smokes."

"Stunning!" added letter B.

Blue Nile Falls / ዓባይ (a-BUY)

this meandering timeless beast seems to roll with a style,
bringing gifts of plentiful water, fertile soil for the Nile.
cascading, whooshing, gushing, roaring waterfall,
keeps nourishing, splashing, toppling off the cliff wall.

ሁ /kuh/ ኩ /koo/ ኪ /kee/ ካ /kah/ ኬ /kay/ ህ /keh/ ኮ /koh/

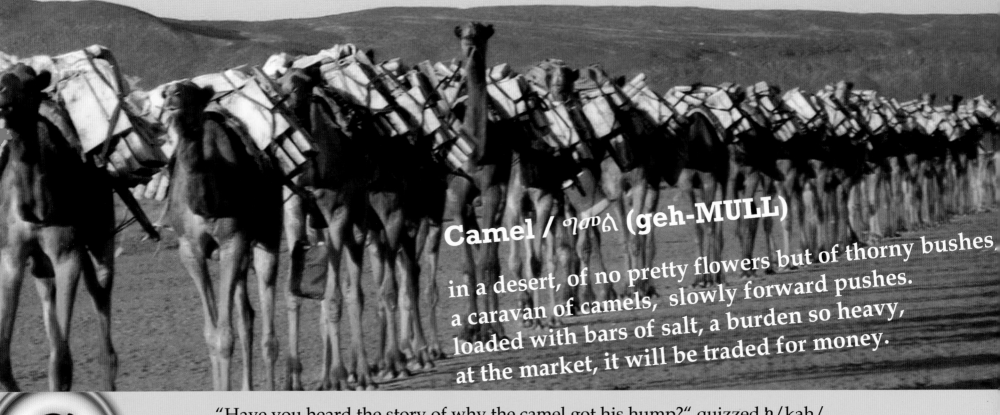

Camel / ግመል (geh-MULL)

in a desert, of no pretty flowers but of thorny bushes,
a caravan of camels, slowly forward pushes.
loaded with bars of salt, a burden so heavy,
at the market, it will be traded for money.

"Have you heard the story of why the camel got his hump?" quizzed ካ /kah/.

"I know it is not to store water," letter C replied with a wink. "Do you know why camels are called 'the ships of a desert?'" said ኬ /kay/ who decided to join the quiz wagon.

Letter C gave a clever response, "When camels walk, they move both legs on one side of their body and then the other. This slow leg movement makes a swaying, rocking motion much like that of a ship on water. That is why."

Impressed, ኩ /koo/ continued, "Out here in the desert, under the burning sun,
live the people of Afar and their loyal friends, their camels.
With no one place to call home, the Afar people live a nomadic lifestyle."

"Ships Ahoy," said C with command.

Dd

D tagged along with the ረ/duh/ letter family. They are in the town of Dessie. Around here, spontaneous dancing to the rhythm of music is a normal event.

"We never need an excuse to sing and dance," said the youngest member, also known as ረ/doh/. She strapped the hand-made drum on her shoulder and began making a joyful sound. A song about new beginnings for the new year.

"I sing alone or we sing together, you see, these songs are like a tether, binding us forever. If it's not one thing, it's another. We sing for joy. We sing for sorrow. We sing for today and for tomorrow."

"Delightful!" said D.

ረ/duh/ ዱ/doo/ ዲ/dee/
ዳ/dah/ ዴ/day/ ደ/deh/
ዶ/doh/

Drum / ከበሮ (kuh-burrow)

a tap, a bang and a boom with the hand,
makes a joyful noise, a beautiful sound.
a beat, a pulse, a rhythm, crisp and loud,
heals the spirit and warms the heart.

Eucalyptus Tree /
የባሕር ዛፍ (yebba-HER zaf)

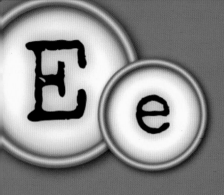

እ/eh/

"Dare, double dare" joked adventurous እ/eh/,
challenging letter E to a run up Mount Entoto, the highest point of AddisAbaba.

The people call it "the city's roof top."
There lies a grand view of a forest densely covered by eucalyptus trees.

Letter E enjoyed the view courtesy of Emperor Menilik,
who founded this city of rolling hills.

Short of breath, E said "I love the smell of these
Eucalyptus trees. Nothing like a breath of fresh air!"

F f

ፉ/fuh/ ፋ/foo/ ፊ/fee/ ፈ/fah/ ፌ/fay/ ፍ/feh/ ፎ/foh/

Flag / ሰንደቅ ዓላማ
(sen-DEK alah-MA)

three horizontal stripes and a star,
green is for hope,
gold is for peace and harmony,
and red for the strength of its people.

"This old flag is Africa's pride," explained
the friendly ፉ/fuh/ with an aura of confidence
and a nose slightly perked up in the air.

"It is the symbol of our identity,
as a never colonized entity,
so we salute and guard it with dignity."

ፌ/fay/ felt like more needed to be said,
"A motherland of heroes kept the
country's freedom ringing
from its mountain tops, to its valleys, rivers
and virgin lands."

"I respect that," said F with sincerity.

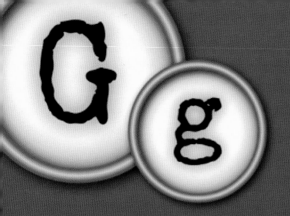

The candy-cane-looking ገ/gah/ challenged G to its favorite game, *Gebeta*. Letter **G** knew this game by the name of *Mancala*.

Nothing like a wooden board game to connect new friends.

They enjoyed the afternoon while sitting at the porch of a hotel with a grand view of the medieval castles of *Gondar*.

"Simply, beautiful," said G.

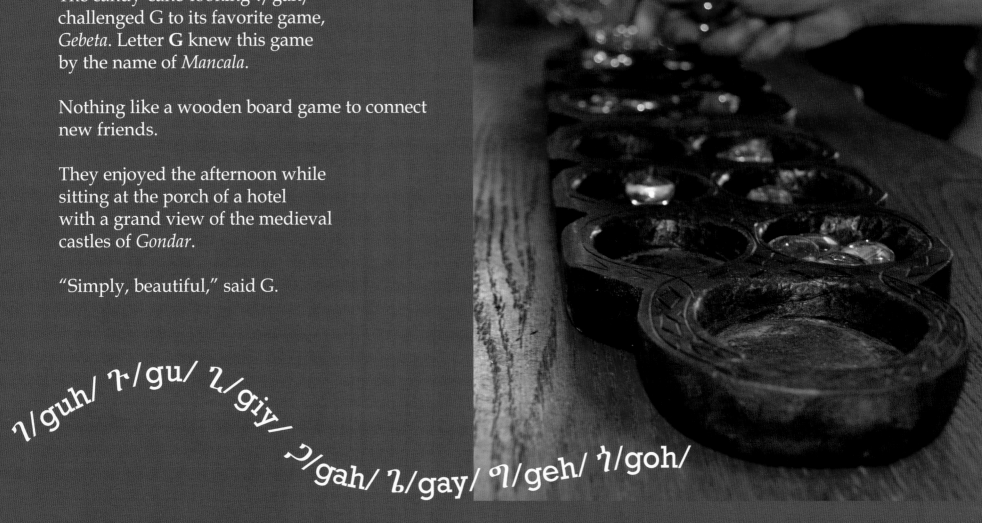

ግ/guh/ ጉ/gu/ ጊ/giy/ ጋ/gah/ ጌ/gay/ ግ/geh/ ጎ/goh/

Gondar / ጎንደር (gone-DUR)

kings and queens once roamed here,
a fortress of power built as empire.
six castles lie in this royal enclosure,
magestic grandeur, glorious fixture.

ሐ/huh/ ሑ/hoo/ ሒ/hee/ ሓ/hah/ ሔ/hay/ ሕ/heh/ ሖ/hoh/

H h

"Wait till you see this old walled city called *Harrar*," remarked the upside-down-fork-looking letter ሐ/huh/.

No room for family pictures and no need for china cabinets. The walls of the homes are decorated with colorfully painted plates and woven baskets.

Home / ቤት (beT)

"In this town," ሑ/hoo/ added,
"you can even witness wild hyenas being fed supper by the local people. Please don't ask me why.
Go ask your fellow tourists."

"Interesting," said H.

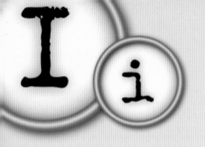

I i

Injera / እንጀራ (in-JEHRA)

ዒ/ee/ and ኢ/ee/

"My grandma is making my favorite dish for dinner. Come along and take your taste buds for a wild ride," insisted letter ዒ/ee/.

An aroma of spices greeted their noses at the door. Letter I watched as the family gathered around a colorful woven basket called *Mesob*. A pancake-like bread called *Injera* with spicy stew called *Doro Wot* was served.

"We invite you to sit down," grandma said. "Here, we use our God-given forks to eat." She used her fingers to roll up a piece of *Injera* to feed the guest.

"This act of feeding is called *gursha*, a sign of friendliness and affection."

After the big meal, letter I joined the coffee ceremony in a room filled with incense, a tradition preserved for centuries.

Letter I was filled with grateful eyes.

J j

Ɉ/juh/ Ɉ/joo/ Ɉ/jee/ Ɉ/jah/ Ɉ/jay/ Ɉ/jeh/ Ɉ/joh/

"I will be your guide to the 'eat this, not that' of Ethiopian spices," said Ɉ/joh/. His chest jutted out with pride at the fancy way he is written.

"Our healthy food will make you smile.
We cook juicy veggies in bite-sized pieces.
And we add spice to every dish.
Spiced-up butter, spiced-up bread.
Wouldn't you know it, there is even a spiced-up tea.

But, be careful as you approach your food.
Be especially aware of the red stuff,
otherwise known as the "spice of life."
This chief spice is not ginger or cardamom,
No, no. It is not nutmeg or cumin or coriander.
The king of spices is the mixture called *berbere*.
Full of heat, it will make your taste buds jump.
Your first taste of *berbere* is an experience you will just simply never forget."

J dared to try a bit of *berbere* and cried, "hot!".
"Don't say I didn't warn you," remarked Ɉ/joh/.

Jalapeño Pepper Spice

ቃርያ (QA-REE-ya)   በርበሬ (BRR-BER-ay)   ቅመም (keh-MUM)

a special blend of leaves and seeds,
dried tree barks, roots, and stems.
chopped, mixed, mushed, well grounded,
to create tasteful, delightful food, indeed.

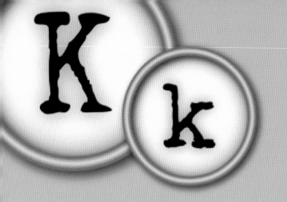

Letter K and ከ/kah/ were visiting while sitting on a three-legged wooden stools. Suddenly ከ/kah/ started to reminisce, "when I was growing up as a little girl, with braided hair and all, I loved going to *Kes Timehirtbet* (a Priest School). I used to walk to school with my friends ጆ/joh/, ቢ/bee/ and ሊ/lee/. I learned how to read there.

At the end of each priest school day, I would run back home, eager to help my mother do her chores.

Sometimes, my mother would give me a penny, and I would run to the neighborhood *suk*, the one-window, one-room grocery store, to buy a candy named *Desta Keremela* (Happy Candy). I used to really enjoy happy candy!"

"What a treat it must have been," reflected letter K.

ከ/kuh/ ኩ/koo/ ኪ/kee/ ከ/kah/ ኬ/kay/ ከ/keh/ ኮ/koh/

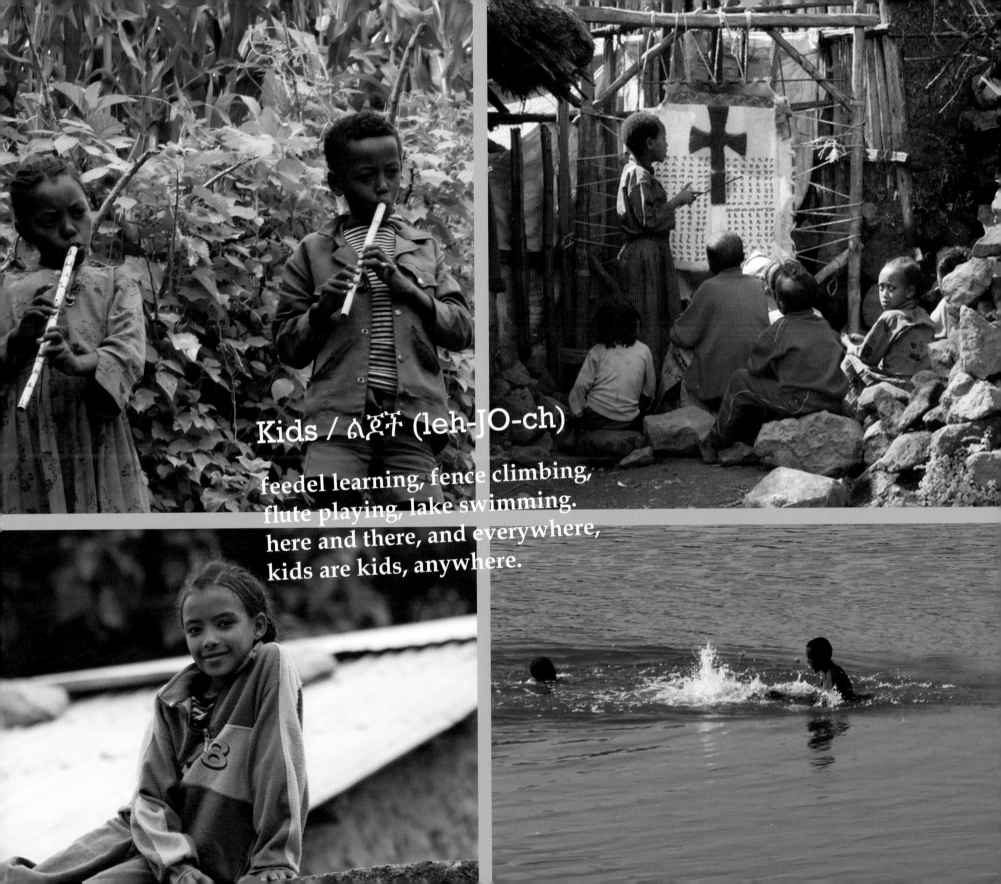

Kids / ልጆች (leh-JO-ch)

feedel learning, fence climbing,
flute playing, lake swimming.
here and there, and everywhere,
kids are kids, anywhere.

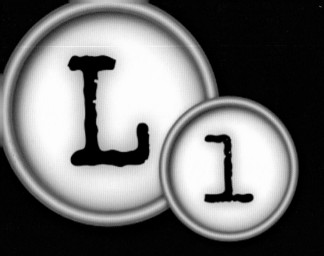

L l

ለ/luh/ ሉ/loo/ ሊ/lee/ ላ/lah/ ሌ/lay/ ል/leh/ ሎ/loh/

It is early morning in *Bahir Dar*,
the city where the ለ/luh/ Feedel family lives.

As the sunlight shone through the morning sky,
ሎ/loh/ jumped out of his bed
excited to load up his boat made of papyrus.
"It is time for a boat ride," he announced
steering the boat towards the peninsula,
on Lake *Tana*.

"In this small corner of this big lake,
lies the headwaters,
the beginning of the world's longest
and winding river called the Nile."

L enjoyed the fresh air,
feeling the light breeze on his face
and watching a flock of pelicans."

Lake Tana / ጣና ሐይቅ (tana-hike)

dotted with peaceful islands of monks,
sprinkled with coffee plants along its banks,
a sight of sleeping hippos, white pelicans in flocks,
a highway for fishermen in papyrus boats.

Monkey / ዝንጀሮ (zIN-JERO)

a glimpse of a wild monkey
roaming free in coffee country
sitting on a tree with both feet
may be searching for a treat to eat

መ/muh/ ሙ/moo/ ሚ/mee/ ማ/mah/ ሜ/may/ ም/meh/ ሞ/moh/

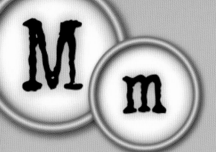

መ/muh/ took a closer look at his family's guest and said, "You almost look like me."
M replied, "Except I thought you looked like a pair of sunglasses." They both giggled.

"There is so much to see and so much to do," መ/muh/ said.
"Would you like to see the mischief of monkeys? They do mischief a lot!
Or may be you want to hear a roaring lion with black mane."
Letter M scratched his head. መ/muh/ decided for the both of them.

"Why not shop at the biggest open market in Africa, the *Merkato*?
It is so big, it is like a city. Whatever you are looking for, chances are you will find it there!"

M bought some gifts of wood carvings, traditional woven clothes, and spices. "Marvelous choices," said his new friend.

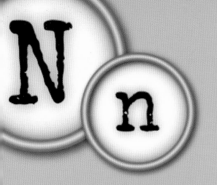

N n

Name / ስም (seM)

"Hello, my name is ኖ/noh/," said a voice near N's ear.

"I am a letter. But if you ask anyone around here, 'what is in a name?' they will say 'everything.'

My name might tell you what town I come from, what language I speak and what religion my parents believe. Interesting?" queried ኖ/noh/.

"No kidding," said letter N.

"It gets better. We have no family names. Instead, I am known through my father's family tree. A child is expected to grow up memorizing his ancestor's names up to seven generations.

Do you name your children after your country?" "No," said N.

"Here we do. Ethiopia is a girl's name," ኖ/noh/ gave a proud nod.

Kokebe [My star]

Bereket [Blessings]

Ashenafi [winner]

Negest [queen]

Genet [paradise]

Tigist [patience]

Teshome [appointed]

Selamawit [peaceful]

Zahra [white flower]

Nahom [compassionate]

Obelisk / ሐውልት (how-will-IT)

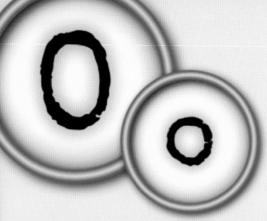

ዖ/oh/ ኦ/oh/

ኦ/oh/ leaned forward, remembering...

"I live in the city now, but my memories
will always lead me home
to the town of *Bati*, my birth place
where everybody knows my name.

This is where it took a village to raise me.
My oldest sister used to braid my hair.
My friends and I used to follow the river banks
to collect firewood for cooking.
And when we returned, my neighbor,
Emama Taitu, used to feed us freshly baked bread.

We would then play the day away at my uncle's farm
skipping rope and swinging on tree swings.

Oh! I miss those days."

Painting / ሥዕል (SEE-EL)

ፐ/puh/ ፑ/poo/ ፒ/pee/ ፓ/pah/ ፔ/pay/ ፕ/peh/ ፖ/poh/

"They say 'a picture is worth a thousand words'. Just look at this painting," said ፖ/poh/.

"Once upon a time, a very very long time ago, there used be a painter who painted the church walls and ceilings, all over town. He painted stories from the Bible.

He named this painting 'The Holy Trinity.' Would you believe it? That was 500 years ago, in the 16th century. He painted stories of Noah and of David and Goliath, telling stories with no words.

He kept painting stories for the church people. The people learned, memorized and kept the stories alive for their children, their grandchildren and their great grandchildren and so it goes."

"What a way to preserve customs and traditions!"
P was properly impressed.

Makeda, the Queen of Sheba Doll from EthiDolls collections.

"We are in *Hadar*," said ቅ/qah/
with a quiet smile.
"A city deep in the Rift Valley.
The first humans lived here, including Lucy."

"Who is Lucy?" asked Q.
"Lucy was one of the first women.
Her bones rested here for some 3 million years!

Much of what people know about early
humans, they learned from studying Lucy.
Those humans walked upright and ate mostly
plants, fruit, nuts and roots.
Maybe Lucy was their queen."

"Quite enchanting," said Q, he felt like he had
traveled back in time, walking on the footprints
of his ancestors.

ቁ/quh/ ቁ/qoo/ ቄ/qee/ ቃ/qah/ ቄ/qay/ ቅ/qeh/ ቆ/qoh/

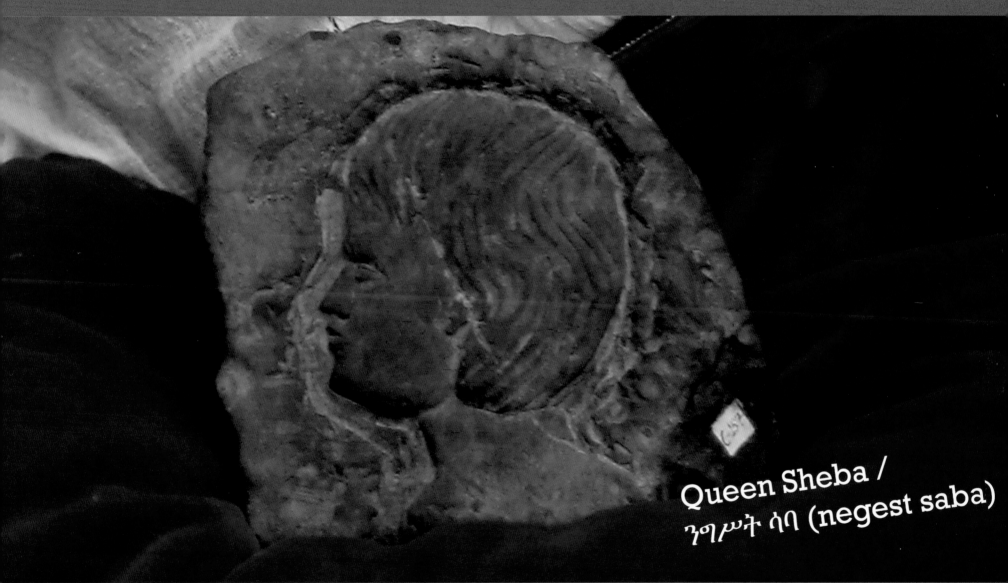

Queen Sheba /
ንግሥት ሳባ (negest saba)

Stone engravings of what is thought to be of Queen Sheba from the church of Saint Mary of Zion in Axum, Ethiopia.

Runner / ሩጫ (RWA-ch)

ሪ/ruh/ ሩ/roo/ ሪ/ree/ ራ/rah/ ሬ/ray/ ር/reh/ ሮ/roh/

"Born to run? Fit to run? Not I," said the slightly rounded ራ/rah/.

"But this East African nation has some of the greatest distance runners of all time.
For them winning races is everything.
One leg in front of another,
over the hills, across the plains,
in the rain and against the wind,
with shoes or without,
beginners or professionals, girls and boys alike.
They never rest. They keep on running."

With that, ሮ/roh/ rushed letter R off to the town
of *Begoji* to see a river of runners.
"Off and running", said R.

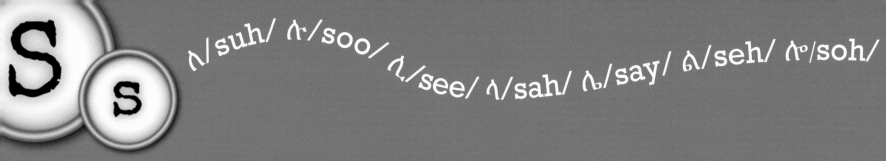

S s

ሰ /suh/ ሱ /soo/ ሲ /see/ ሳ /sah/ ሴ /say/ ስ /seh/ ሶ /soh/

"I must tell you something!" said short legged ስ/soh/ eagerly.

"Soccer is the most adored sport in Ethiopia.
Here, we call it football. Kind of makes sense if you ask me," teased ስ/soh/.

Sunday afternoon finds the ስ/soh/ letter family and many others at the stadium cheering for their favorite team.

The sights and sounds of the city, the bright smiles of the children and the sparkle in their eyes make any day look brighter.

S knew it would all stay in his mind even after he left the country.

Soccer / የእግር ኳስ
(YEA-EGR-kwas)

Tukul / ጎጆ (gojo)

ተ/tuh/ ቱ/too/ ቲ/tee/ ታ/tah/ ቴ/tay/ ት/teh/ ቶ/toh/

T t

"Have you ever seen tukuls?" asked the curious ታ/tah/.
"I'm sure I have not," replied T.

"Don't worry," said ታ/tah/. "We've got you covered. Just look around you.

Tukuls are round huts built with mud and sticks.
They have dirt floors. The roofs are made out of dried grass.
Sometimes, the inside walls are decorated with old newspapers.

I used to play 'I spy' games with my brothers
using the headlines on the wall."

"I am sure that was a lot of fun!" said T.

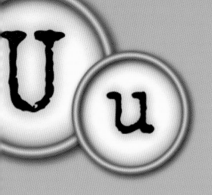

ዩ/yoo/

"The really smart kids go to this university campus behind these big gates.
It is called Addis Ababa University," said ዩ/yoo/.

"It is special to be a student there.
Students are expected to read lots of books and study really hard;
otherwise there won't be a spot available for them next semester.

It is cool to be in school, and their parents are full of pride!"

"I understand," said U.

University /
ዩኒቨርሲቲ (Uni-versity)

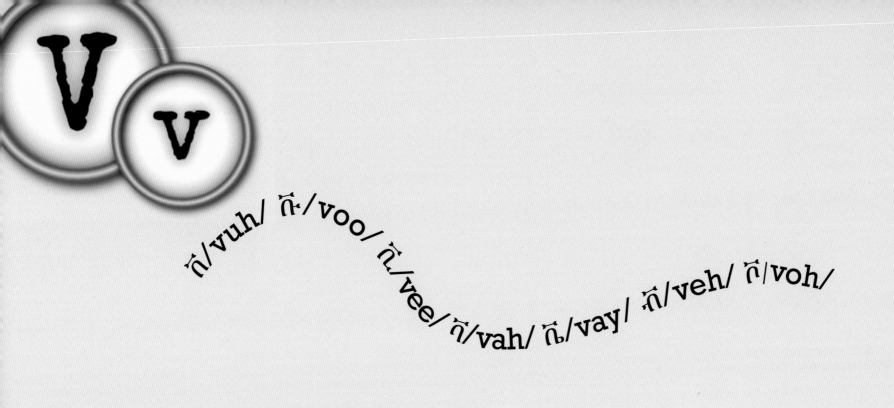

"This sight will rock your world!" said ñ/vay/ excitedly.

"We are at one of the hottest places on earth. *Erta Ale* is the name of this spectacular volcanic lava lake."

"Wow, what does that mean?" asked V.

ñ/vee/ chimed in. "It means 'smoking mountain' in the language of the Afar, the people who live here.
Around here, rainfall is a rare event.
And every night is a fireworks night with a fountain of fire shooting to the sky.
An amazing display of erupting lights provided by mother nature."

V's interest was piqued.
He couldn't wait to share this story with his friends back home.

Volcano / የእሳት ነመራ
(YEA-sat GO-mera)

deep beneath the earth, heated by boiling lava,
is a sea of molten rock, fountain of red hot magma.

Ɯ/wuh/ Ɯ/woo/ Ɯ/wee/ Ɯ/wah/ Ɯ/way/ Ɯ/weh/ Ɯ/woh/

"Weaving, weaving, everywhere!
Weaving baskets, weaving gourds,
Weaving hats and weaving dresses,
Weaving on roofs and weaving on horses.
Looks like the art of weaving has gone crazy.
Weaving, weaving, everywhere! "
sang Ɯ/wee/ with glee,
showing off his rookie rhyming skill.

"Wow," said W.

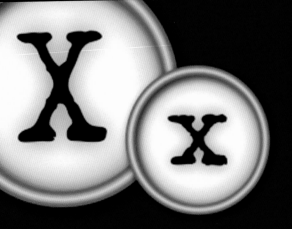

ኤክስ /x/

"Ethiopia is the land of eXtremes,
eXtremes of the lands," eXplained the letters
ኤክስ /x/.

"Opposing things living side by side,
I will show you urban dwellings and rural huts,
rough roads and modern, zippy ones,
very hot deserts and chilly highlands,
noisy singing in the middle of calm devotions,
high mountains and the lowest point on Earth,
wild creatures and domesticated ones,
cell phones and oXen-pulled plows.

Ethiopia has city people and those living in
ancient ways,
new ways of thinking with old traditional life.
All eXtremes are on display here."
X was eXcited to see it all.

EXtreme Devotion /መትጋት (mET-gat)

Y y

የ/yuh/ ዩ/yoo/ ዪ/yee/ ያ/yah/ ዬ/yay/ ይ/yeh/ ዮ/yoh/

Yellow Flower /
አደይ አበባ (YA-day Abeba)

"September is here, my favorite time of the year!" said ዮ/yoh/.
"The old year is out. The new year is in. A fresh new start for every living being.
The heavy rain has stopped. The sun is shining and the grass is growing.
But I especially love the flowers blooming. Little yellow Meskal daisies carpeting the scene.
Little boys giving out gifts of colorful spring painting.
Beautifully dressed little girls go caroling, singing
"*Abebayehosh*" and beating the drum. And the bells in my heart go ringing.
Shall we go outside and have some fun?" "You bet," said letter Y excitedly.

The guest letters were full of sights, sounds,
smells, tastes and textures.
They felt positively zingy.

Z stepped forward to speak for everyone.
"We have come to the end of our journey."
All of you have been gracious hosts,
and we appreciate your hospitality.
In fact, we have fallen in love with your country."

Good old ዙ/zoo/ cleared his throat.
"Of course! It was our pleasure!
Should you have second thoughts about needing to go,
please stay on as our guests as long as you wish.
Together, we all make words that open up the world
and give us all a zest for learning more."

As the taxis zoomed off for the airport,
the letters of the alphabet knew they would
always be part of Ethiopia now. And Ethiopia would
be part of them.

Feedel and Alphabet. Alphabet and Feedel.

Friends forever!

Goodbye /ደህና ሁኑ/

ዝ/zuh/ ዙ/zoo/ ዚ/zee/ ዛ/zah/ ዜ/zay/ ዝ/zeh/ ዞ/zoh/

Zebra / የሜዳ አህያ (YEA-ME-da-ahi-ya)

Gratitude

My utmost respect and gratitude goes to my mentor and my friend, Jane Kurtz, who is one of the great ambassadors of world literacy. This book is dedicated to the children of Ethiopia who blossom when given an opportunity. An opportunity to read books, learn in schools and read in libraries. Cultivating minds for a stronger tomorrow is the work of Ethiopia Reads, a non-profit organization based in the United States.

My special thanks goes to the people who graciously allowed me to use their finest works of art, their photographs. I especially would like to thank Marlys Brown, Ron Gronneberg, Semehar Tesfaye, Stephanie Schlatter, Stijn Luyck, Yohannes Aychew and the good people at Awura Tour and Travel Agency.

I would also like to extend my gratitude to the wonderful people who have helped me throughout the book writing process, by providing support, proofreading and editing. Thank you to Berhanu Assefa, Sheri Fercho, Leanne Gronneberg, Jane Kurtz, Amy Richardson and Mavis Siem.

Grateful for my partner in life, my love, my husband and my friend, Ron. My parents, Asamenech and Abera, for their constant encouragement and prayers.

To the letters of the Amharic Feedel for being my first window to the written world.

Special Attribution of Photographs

Front Cover: BMC Ecology image competition 2014: the winning images. BMC Ecology 2014, Ryan J. Burke (University of Oxford)

Back Cover: Erta Ale, shield volcano in the Danakil Depression of the Afar Region of northeastern Ethiopia - Awura Tour and Travel Agency

Alise Osis for kids eating Injera and wot
Ayanna Nahmias for the young girls celebrating Asheda in Tigray
Awura Tour and Travel Agency for Gelada Baboons and Camel carvans
Ethidolls.com for Makeda, Queen of Sheba Doll
Ethiopian Airlines for the Ethiopian Airline flight crew
Ethiopia Reads for the decorated horse (www.ethiopiareads.org)
Matt Andrea for Erta Ale volcano
Yohannes Aychew, for pelicans on Lake Tana